HOW TO DEAL

ANGER DANGER

MICHELLE GARCIA ANDERSEN

rourkeeducationalmedia.com

SCHOOL to HOME
CONNECTIONS

BEFORE AND DURING READING ACTIVITIES

Before Reading: *Building Background Knowledge and Vocabulary*

Building background knowledge can help children process new information and build upon what they already know. Before reading a book, it is important to tap into what children already know about the topic. This will help them develop their vocabulary and increase their reading comprehension.

Questions and Activities to Build Background Knowledge:

1. Look at the front cover of the book and read the title. What do you think this book will be about?
2. What do you already know about this topic?
3. Take a book walk and skim the pages. Look at the table of contents, photographs, captions, and bold words. Did these text features give you any information or predictions about what you will read in this book?

Vocabulary: *Vocabulary Is Key to Reading Comprehension*

Use the following directions to prompt a conversation about each word.

- Read the vocabulary words.
- What comes to mind when you see each word?
- What do you think each word means?

WITHDRAWN

Vocabulary Words:
- assertive
- depression
- impulse
- meditation
- precedes
- preventative
- reconcile
- self-esteem
- strategies
- suppressing
- triggers
- vent

During Reading: *Reading for Meaning and Understanding*

To achieve deep comprehension of a book, children are encouraged to use close reading strategies. During reading, it is important to have children stop and make connections. These connections result in deeper analysis and understanding of a book.

 Close Reading a Text

During reading, have children stop and talk about the following:

- Any confusing parts
- Any unknown words
- Text to text, text to self, text to world connections
- The main idea in each chapter or heading

Encourage children to use context clues to determine the meaning of any unknown words. These strategies will help children learn to analyze the text more thoroughly as they read.

When you are finished reading this book, turn to page 46 for **Text-Dependent Questions** and an **Extension Activity**.

TABLE OF CONTENTS

CHAPTER 1

WHAT IS ANGER?

Kira spent the entire summer training for soccer. She was determined to be the starting goalie this year. The week before tryouts, she and a few friends went to the park to practice. The field was uneven and badly needed mowing. When the ball sped past the sweeper and headed for the goal, Kira lunged and her foot caught in the tall grass. She heard a snap as she collapsed on the ground. As she waited at the hospital for treatment for her broken ankle, Kira felt some pain. She felt some frustration. But mostly, she felt angry!

It is common to feel angry when we experience deep disappointment. People get angry for many reasons. Sometimes it is an external reason, like when someone offends you with their words or actions. Other times we feel anger internally when we let ourselves down.

People often try to avoid feeling angry. However, anger is a natural emotion and when handled appropriately has many benefits. It alerts us when we feel threatened by signaling the fight-or-flight response. It can inspire us to think creatively to **reconcile** problems and make changes. Anger is a powerful motivator, and it can help us reach our goals.

Fight-or-Flight

Fight-or-flight *is a term used to describe one way our bodies react to stress. Our brain acts as an alarm, flooding our systems with hormones and physiological changes. This prepares us to either fight the threat or take flight and head for safety.*

The key to anger is learning how to control it before it controls you. There are many **strategies** that teach us how to deal with our anger in healthy ways. One helpful strategy is journaling.

A New Way to Journal

Many people like electronic journals. With a journaling app, you can include photos and posts from your social media accounts. Look for an app that is password protected, can sync from any device, is user-friendly, and has easy exporting in case you change to a different app later on.

Journaling has many positive health benefits. When we write about our anger, it can reduce the intensity of our emotions and relieve our stress. With less stress, our moods improve, and our happiness increases. Journaling helps us become more in tune with our thoughts and emotions. It also improves memory.

Get Creative

Some people prefer drawing about their feelings instead of writing about them. Expressing one's emotions through art can be therapeutic. Try creating an art journal and draw, paint, or collage how you feel. There's no wrong way to do it

CHAPTER 2

YOUR BODY'S REACTION TO ANGER

Nathan's football team had just lost their first game in an undefeated season. He went into the locker room and threw his helmet on the ground. He could feel his heart racing. He was sweating and every muscle tensed. His coach told him to walk it off, but he couldn't calm down. He felt out of control. Then someone made a joke about them losing. Nathan exploded and punched a hole in the wall.

Our bodies give us warning signs as our anger escalates. Learning to recognize these signs and practicing **impulse** control can help keep our anger from turning to fury. It is difficult to think rationally when we are seething with anger. Sometimes the wisest thing we can do is remove ourselves from the situation that is causing our anger before reacting to it.

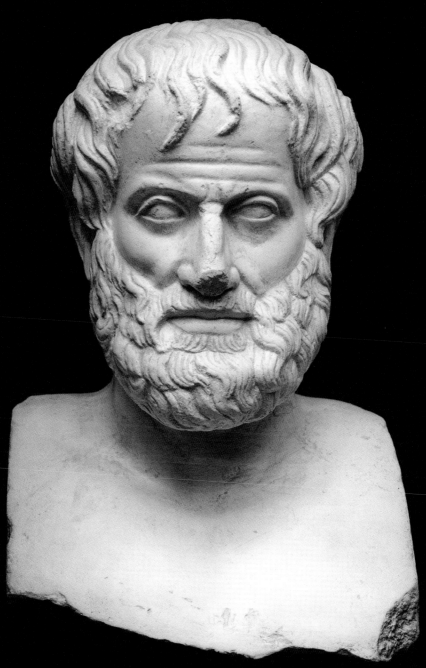

Greek philosopher Aristotle once said,

"Anybody can become angry—that is easy, but to be angry with the right person, and to the right degree, at the right time, and for the right purpose, and in the right way—that is not within everybody's power and is not easy."

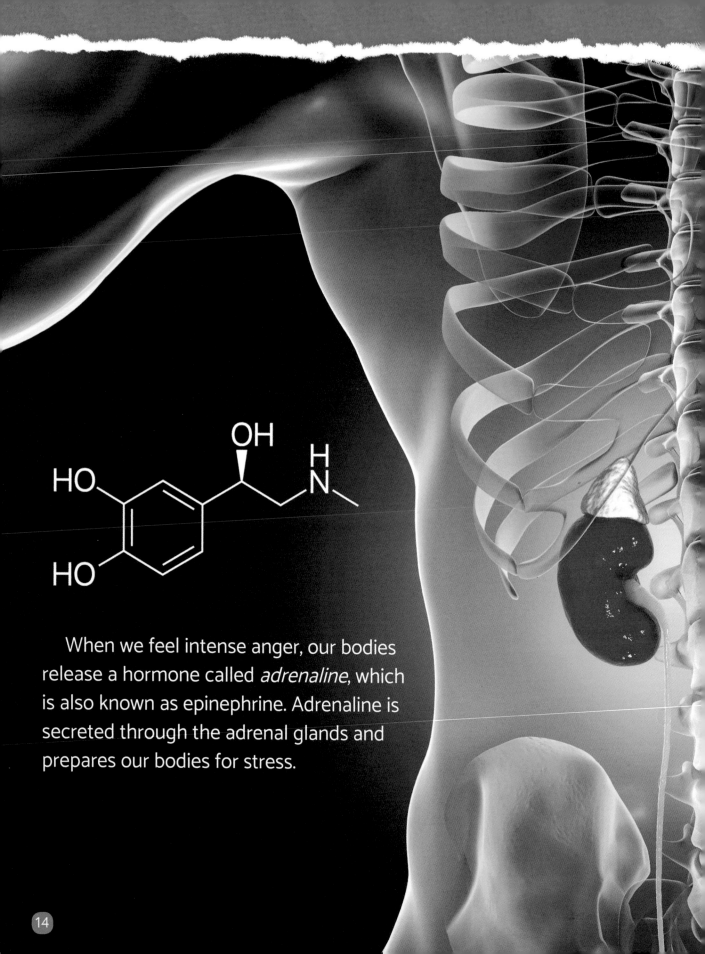

When we feel intense anger, our bodies release a hormone called *adrenaline*, which is also known as epinephrine. Adrenaline is secreted through the adrenal glands and prepares our bodies for stress.

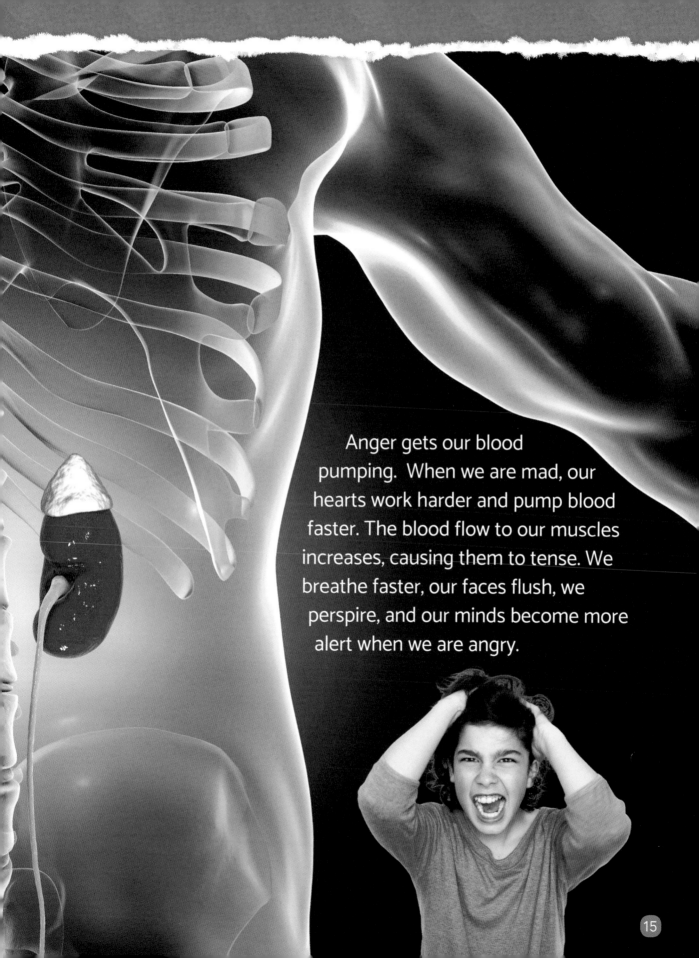

Anger gets our blood pumping. When we are mad, our hearts work harder and pump blood faster. The blood flow to our muscles increases, causing them to tense. We breathe faster, our faces flush, we perspire, and our minds become more alert when we are angry.

When you feel adrenaline surging through you, try working it off by doing something physical. Riding your bike, running, dancing, or hitting a punching bag can help you to release built-up tension in your body and relieve your stress. Exercise is a great **preventative** to explosive anger.

Don't Forget to Laugh

Did you know that one of the quickest ways to defuse anger is with humor? The next time you feel yourself getting angry, try to lighten the mood with a joke.

CHAPTER 3

EXPRESSING ANGER

Mia's mom said she could invite only five friends over for a sleepover. Mia knew exactly who she would invite—the same five girls she'd hung out with since grade school. Mia especially wanted to spend time with her best friend, Sophie. Since starting middle school, Sophie hadn't been around much; she seemed to be making new friends.

When Mia invited Sophie to her party, she agreed to come only if she could invite her new friend Emily too. Mia had to choose: Either take one of her longtime friends off the guest list or risk her best friend not coming to her party. Mia didn't like the way Sophie pressured her. For the first time, she was angry with her best friend.

It's natural to get angry when we feel pressured to do something we don't want to do. We may be tempted to lash out at the person who angers us. However, engaging in verbal insults only makes the problem worse. It is best to take a moment and think before saying something you might regret.

Nonverbal Communication

Did you know you can say a lot without any words? Pay attention to your body language. Furrowed eyebrows, pursed lips, glaring eyes, and crossed arms are just some of the ways we reveal our anger. If you want to improve your body language, practice in front of a mirror.

There is nothing wrong with being **assertive** and standing up for yourself. When expressing anger, try to keep calm. Practice being a good listener and try being open-minded. Respond with personal statements like, *"I feel angry when you pressure me to do things I don't want to."* Don't use generalizations like, *"You always do that!"*

No matter how angry you are, don't give ultimatums or make demands. Instead of saying, *"You better not do that again or we will no longer be friends,"* try saying things like, *"I would prefer you not do that again."*

Being a good communicator is an important life skill. Practice getting your point across without losing your temper.

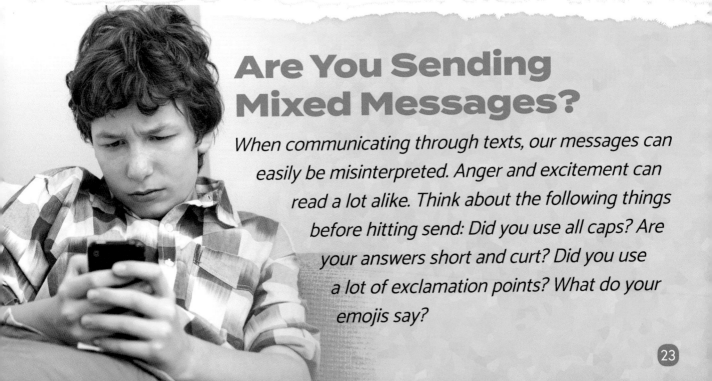

Are You Sending Mixed Messages?

When communicating through texts, our messages can easily be misinterpreted. Anger and excitement can read a lot alike. Think about the following things before hitting send: Did you use all caps? Are your answers short and curt? Did you use a lot of exclamation points? What do your emojis say?

CHAPTER 4

>>> >< < > < >< <

SUPPRESSING ANGER

>>> >< < > >< <

**M**atteo was too old for toys, but he kept a few from his childhood hidden beneath his bed. His favorite was a Transformer he built out of Legos. Since Matteo hadn't played with toys in years, his mom thought nothing of it when she found the Transformer and gave it to his little brother, who completely disassembled it in seconds.

When Matteo saw what his brother had done, he was furious. He wanted to tell his mom how it made him feel. But because he thought he was too old for toys, he was embarrassed and kept his anger to himself.

Sometimes we have difficulty expressing our anger, and instead, hold on to it and keep it to ourselves. **Suppressing** our anger temporarily has some advantages. It allows us time to cool down and think rationally. Sometimes this cooling-off period is just what we need to turn our anger into something constructive.

However, there are risks associated with suppressing our anger for too long. When we don't open up about how we feel, it causes a buildup of stress inside of us. Eventually, we reach a breaking point, and sometimes we end up exploding in anger and hurting the people we love.

Anger Affects More Than Our Moods

*Holding on to anger causes physical side effects. Listen to your body and learn to recognize the symptoms, which can include upset stomach, headaches, sleeplessness, anxiety, and **depression**. Anger can also cause high blood pressure and trigger heart attacks and strokes.*

"Holding on to anger is like grasping a hot coal with the intent of throwing it at someone else; you are the one who gets burned."
—Buddha

Unmanaged anger causes mood swings and lowers our **self-esteem**. Perhaps we act out as a way of getting back. Instead, we should try to identify why we are angry and make a plan to fix what's bothering us. Communicating our feelings in a healthy way prevents long-term anger, which can lead to depression.

Super Sad?
There's Help

Sometimes, you might feel alone and think that everyone is against you. You might experience low moods, which can lead to thoughts of self-harm or suicide. Always tell a friend if you feel like harming yourself. Then, tell a trusted adult such as a parent, relative, teacher, clergy member, or medical professional who can help you get the support you need. The National Suicide Prevention Lifeline is available 24 hours a day to provide help at 1-800-273-8255.

CHAPTER 5

CALMING
TECHNIQUES

Isabel and her friends always studied together after school and on weekends. They challenged one another academically and strived to be the best. The girls worked hard preparing for an upcoming math test. The exam would determine their placement for the following school year.

Although Isabel thought she had prepared, the test was more difficult than she expected. Isabel was the only one of her friends not placed in the advanced math class. She felt rejected and angry that one test changed everything. And worse, she was embarrassed to tell her friends.

Being rejected feels very personal because it's a direct hit to our self-esteem. Rejection quite often **precedes** embarrassment, another common cause for anger. Knowing how to cope in these situations takes patience and practice.

To begin, start by taking deep, abdominal breaths. Slowly count while you are breathing. This will help you focus on something other than your anger. Picture yourself in a peaceful place that relaxes you. With concentration, your anger should subside. Many people find yoga and **meditation** relaxing and helpful for dealing with their anger.

Give Meditation a Try

Did you know that people have been meditating for over 5,000 years? Many people all around the world practice the art of meditation. It increases self-awareness and is known to relieve stress. It takes discipline and focus to meditate, but anyone can do it.

Listening to music is another peaceful method for calming down. Try listening to something that will soothe your mind or lift your spirits. Music alone might not be enough to alleviate your anger. If that's the case, take your mind off of things by reading, solving a puzzle, or doing something else that brings you pleasure. It is natural to feel angry with yourself now and then, but it's important to remember to be kind to yourself when this happens.

CHAPTER 6

HEALTHY LIVING

TO REDUCE ANGER

Devin stayed up late playing video games. He planned to get up early and do his homework, but he overslept. He was running late and didn't have time for breakfast. All day long he struggled to concentrate and grew more irritable as the day wore on. By the time he got home from school, and his mom asked about his science test—the test he bombed—his mood went from irritable to full-fledged angry. He knew he had no one to blame but himself.

Being angry with ourselves is often more difficult than being mad at someone else. When someone wrongs us, we can voice our anger and **vent** our frustrations. But when we are at fault, we need to examine our choices and see where we went wrong. This way, we learn from our mistakes and can prevent them from occurring again.

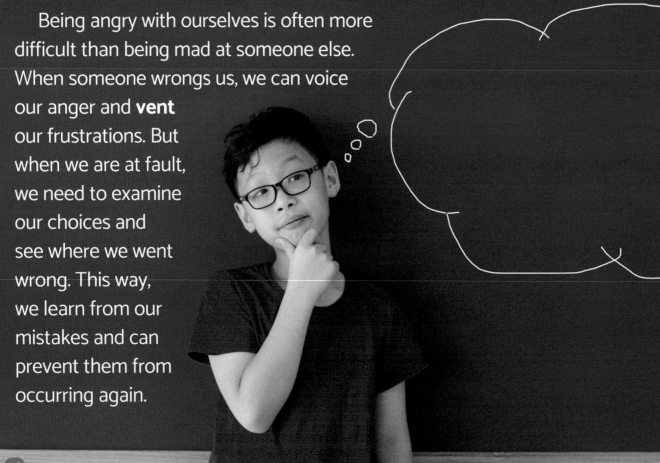

Take a Closer Look

Do you ever find yourself feeling angry for no reason? Sometimes it's our environment and not people that cause our anger. Is the noisy street outside your home aggravating you? Is the hustle and bustle of your daily routine taking a toll? Stop, observe, think, and make changes.

Living a healthy lifestyle can help prevent mood swings that result in anger. For instance, getting plenty of sleep and being rested reduces anxiety. Exercise is not only good for our bodies but our minds as well. Having a clear mind helps us respond to anger with a level head. Eating a healthy diet also

makes a difference. If we fill up on sugary foods and caffeine, we may crash and experience negative mood swings.

Being healthy means making time to do things you enjoy and finding time to relax. Video games are okay, but limit screen time and violent games as they can increase anxiety. Know your **triggers** and try to avoid the things that make you upset when possible. Lastly, make sure you have a supportive group of people you can talk to when you feel yourself struggling with anger.

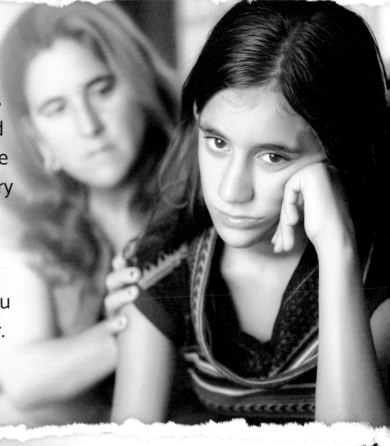

How Much Is Too Much?

The average tween (eight-to-twelve-year-old) spends more than four and a half hours a day on screens. The average teenager spends more than six and a half hours a day on screens. Some screen time promotes creativity. But too much passive, unproductive screen time can lead to irritability and anger.

ACTIVITY

WRITE ABOUT IT

Think of a time when you were really angry. What happened that made you so upset? Were you angry with yourself, with someone you care about, with a stranger, or with something in your environment? Did you lash out physically or verbally? Did you suppress your anger? Remember how you felt in that moment and write about it. Then, describe what you would do differently today. List the strategies you would use to defuse your anger.

> > > < < > > < < <

GLOSSARY

assertive (uh-SUR-tiv): able to behave confidently and express yourself positively

depression (di-PRESH-uhn): a perpetual state of unhappiness

impulse (IM-puhls): the desire to do something suddenly and without much thought

meditation (med-i-TAY-shuhn): the act of remaining quiet and thinking deeply

precedes (pree-SEEDZ): comes before or goes in front of something

preventative (pri-VEN-ta-tiv): a method or strategy to prevent something from happening

reconcile (REK-uhn-sile): to figure out, settle, or resolve

self-esteem (self-i-STEEM): a feeling of pride and respect for yourself

strategies (STRAT-i-jeez): plans or methods for achieving goals

suppressing (suh-PRES-ing): putting a stop to or preventing something from happening

triggers (TRIG-urz): events or situations that cause something to happen

vent (vent): to release an emotion

INDEX

TEXT-DEPENDENT QUESTIONS

1. What does the term *fight-or-flight* mean?
2. Describe the health benefits of journaling.
3. What is adrenaline?
4. Name three ways our bodies react to anger.
5. Pretend you are Mia. What would you do? Would you invite Sophie's new friend Emily to your party so Sophie would attend?

EXTENSION ACTIVITY

Find a partner and create a scenario that would cause him or her to be angry. How would they deal with the situation? What would they say? What would they do to defuse anger? Once your partner has shared answers, have him or her create a situation for you. What would you say? What would you do?

BIBLIOGRAPHY

Ackerman, Courtney. "83 Benefits of Journaling for Depression, Anxiety, and Stress Management (PDF)." Positive Psychology Program - Your One-Stop PP Resource!. positivepsychologyprogram.com/benefits-of-journaling/. (accessed September 25, 2018).

Alberti, Robert E., and Michael L. Emmons. *Your Perfect Right: Assertiveness and Equality in Your Life and Relationships*. Impact Publishers, 2017.

American Psychological Association. "Controlling Anger Before It Controls You." American Psychological Association. www.apa.org/topics/anger/control.aspx. (accessed September 25, 2018).

Brookshire, Bethany. "Hormone Affects How Teens' Brains Control Emotions." Science News for Students. www.sciencenewsforstudents.org/article/hormone-affects-how-teens-brains-control-emotions. (accessed September 25, 2018).

Jones-Smith, Elsie. *Nurturing Nonviolent Children: A Guide for Parents, Educators, and Counselors*, Praeger Publishers, 2008.

LifeFlow Audio Technology. "History Of Meditation - Mankind's Oldest Getaway." Project Meditation. www.project-meditation.org/mankinds-oldest-getaway/. (accessed September 25, 2018).

Manning-Schaffel, Vivian. "How Being Angry Can (Sometimes) Be Good for You." NBC Better. www.nbcnews.com/better/health/how-being-angry-can-sometimes-be-good-you-ncna801661. (accessed September 25, 2018).

Mayo Clinic. "Anger Management: Your Questions Answered." Mayo Foundation for Medical Education and Research. www.mayoclinic.org/healthy-lifestyle/adult-health/in-depth/anger-management/art-20048149. (accessed September 25, 2018).

Purcell, Maud. "The Health Benefits of Journaling." Psych Central. psychcentral.com/lib/the-health-benefits-of-journaling/. (accessed September 25, 2018).

Robinson, Lawrence, and Jeanne Segal. "Help for Parents of Troubled Teens: Dealing with Anger, Violence, Delinquency, and Other Teen Behavior Problems." Help Guide. www.helpguide.org/articles/parenting-family/helping-troubled-teens.htm. (accessed September 25, 2018).

Victoria State Government. "Anger - How It Affects People." Better Health Channel. www.betterhealth.vic.gov.au/health/healthyliving/anger-how-it-affects-people. (accessed September 25, 2018).

WebMD. "Mental Health and Anger Management." WebMD. www.webmd.com/mental-health-managing-anger#1. (accessed September 25, 2018).

ABOUT THE AUTHOR

Michelle Garcia Andersen lives in southern Oregon with her husband and three kids. She doesn't often get angry, but when she does, she appreciates long walks to help her cool off. Michelle loves yoga and finds it keeps her calm and at peace.

www.rourkeeducationalmedia.com

PHOTO CREDITS: Cover: photo at top © Littlekidmoment, photo at bottom © Dmytro Zinkevych, both cover photos fro Shutterstock.com; Pg.4-5: BDPub-Editorial; Pg.6-7: shutterstock.com | Jeka, shutterstock.com | CREATISTAshutterstock.com | Suzanne Tucker; Pg.8-9: istock.com | Hoaru, istock.com | bowie15, istock.com | Rawpixel; Pg.10-11: Editorial, istock.com | justinkendra-Edictorial; Pg.12-13: shutterstock.com | Elena Elisseeva, shutterstock.com | MidoSemsem.; Pg.14-15: shutterstock.com | Kateryna Kon, istock.com | ELENA ARA OLIVER; Pg:16-17: istock.com | Sasiistock, shutterstock.com | Piotr Wawrzyniuk, istock.com | goldenKB; Pg.18-19: istock.com | Erstudiostok; Pg.20-21: Shutterstock.com | junpinzon, Shutterstock.com | Motortion Films, Shutterstock.com | Motortion Films, shutterstock.com | freeskyline ;Pg.22-23: shutterstock.com | CREATISTA, shutterstock.com Rawpixel.com, shutterstock.com | MAErtek; Pg.24-25: shutterstock.com | IVL; Pg.26-27: istock.com | diego_cervo, istock.com | monkeybusinessimages; Pg.28-29: shutterstock.com | Mike_shots, shutterstock.com | VaLiza; Pg.30-31: istock.com | allensima, istock.com | Tomwang112, shutterstock.com | y NARONGRIT LOKOOLPRAKIT; Pg.32-33: istock.com | gpointstudio; Pg.34-35: istock.com | Wavebreakmedia, shutterstock.com | Africa Studio, shutterstock.com | maximino; Pg.36-37: istock.com | Wavebreakmedia, istock.com | flukyfluky, shutterstock.com | Dmytro Zinkevych; Pg.38-39: istock.com | yacobchuk; Pg.40-41: istock.com | Kobackpacko, istock.com | hjalmeida; Pg.42-43: shutterstock.com | NattapolStudiO, shutterstock.com | Tono Balaguer, istock.com | marilyna, shutterstock.com | Kamira, istock.com | Yalana.

Edited by: Kim Thompson

Produced by Blue Door Education for Rourke Educational Media. Cover and interior design by: Jennifer Dydyk

Library of Congress PCN Data

Anger Danger / Michelle Garcia Andersen
(How to Deal)
ISBN 978-1-73161-489-6 (hard cover)
ISBN 978-1-73161-296-0 (soft cover)
ISBN 978-1-73161-594-7 (e-Book)
ISBN 978-1-73161-699-9 (e-Pub)
Library of Congress Control Number: 2019932374

Rourke Educational Media
Printed in the United States of America,
North Mankato, Minnesota